First Facts™

Our Government

The State Legislative Branch

by Mary Firestone

Consultant:
Jan Goehring
Program Director
National Conference of State Legislatures
Denver, Colorado

Capstone press

Mankato, Minnesota

First Facts is published by Capstone Press
151 Good Counsel Drive, P.O. Box 669, Mankato, Minnesota 56002
http://www.capstonepress.com

Library of Congress Cataloging-in-Publication Data
Firestone, Mary.
    The state legislative branch / by Mary Firestone.
    p. cm.—(First facts. Our government)
    Summary: Introduces the legislative branch of state government, how legislators are
elected, and how a bill becomes law.
    Includes bibliographical references and index.
    ISBN 0-7368-2501-0 (hardcover)
    1. Legislative bodies—United States—States—Juvenile literature. [1. Legislative
bodies—United States—States. 2. Legislators. 3. Legislation. 4. State governments.] I. Title.
II. Series.
JK2488.F58 2004
328.73—dc21   2003011122

Editorial Credits
Christine Peterson, editor; Jennifer Bergstrom, designer; Jo Miller, photo researcher;
    Eric Kudalis, product planning editor

Photo Credits
AP/Wide World Photos/Gregory Smith, 13; Mark Foley, cover; Mike Fuentes, 19; Rogelio Solis, 16
Cindy Reinitz, 5
Corbis/Bettmann, 20; Reuters NewMedia Inc., 14–15; SABA/David Butow, 9
Getty Images Inc./Matt Archer, 10–11
Minnesota Pollution Control Agency, 5 (inset)
Photri-Microstock, 17
Root Resources/D. I. MacDonald, 7

1 2 3 4 5 6 09 08 07 06 05 04

Table of Contents

Children Help Legislators

Minnesota students and **legislators** worked to pass a law to study frogs. Students found frogs that were missing eyes and had extra legs. They told lawmakers about the frogs. Legislators passed a law. The law gave scientists money to learn more about the frogs.

 Fun Fact:
Unusual frogs were found in 35 states. Scientists continue to study the unusual frogs.

State Government

Parts of state government work together. The **executive** branch makes sure laws are followed. The **judicial** branch decides what laws mean.

Parts of State Government

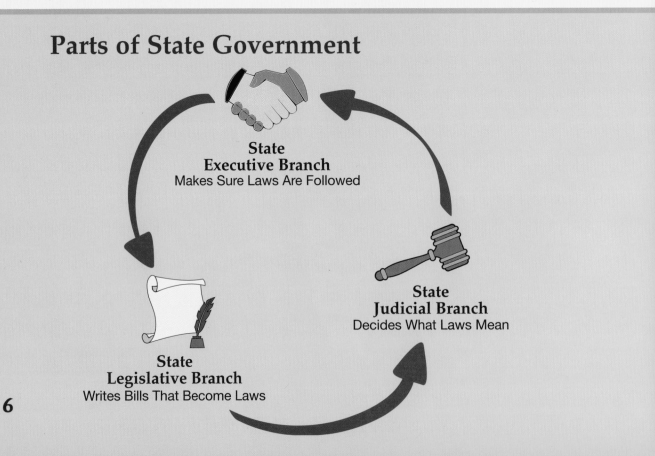

State
Executive Branch
Makes Sure Laws Are Followed

State
Judicial Branch
Decides What Laws Mean

State
Legislative Branch
Writes Bills That Become Laws

Members of a state's **legislative** branch work at the state capitol. The legislative branch writes and passes **bills**. Bills can become state law.

How Legislators Are Elected

Every state is divided into districts. Each district has about the same number of people. People in each district vote for legislators. These leaders serve in the state legislature. State legislators serve **terms** that last two or four years.

 Fun Fact:
In the United States there are 7,382 state legislators.

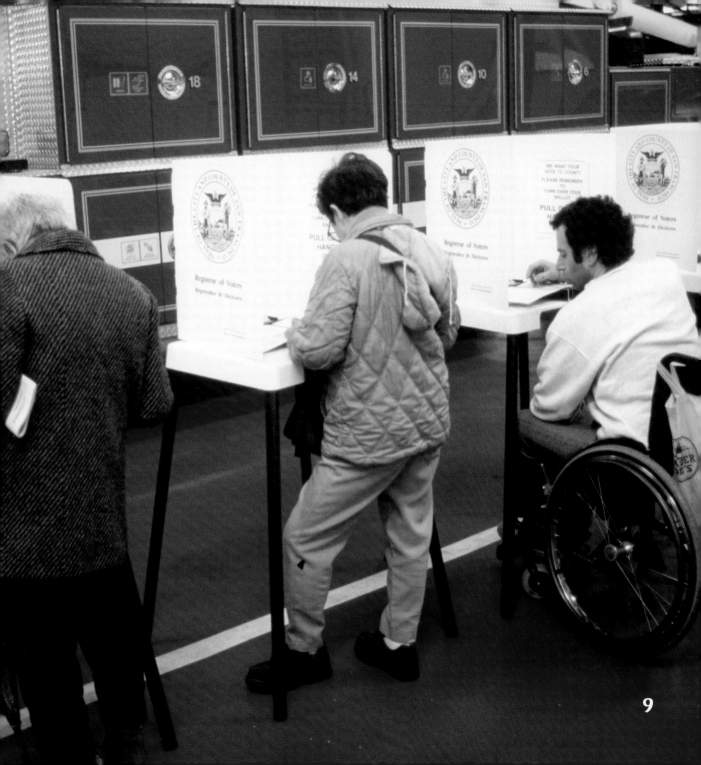

The Number of Legislators

Each state has a different number of legislators. Laws in each state list the number of legislators. Nebraska has the fewest number of legislators with 49. New Hampshire has the most legislators with 424.

Fun Fact:
State legislators must be U.S. citizens. Legislators also must live in the state where they serve.

A Bill Becomes Law

Anyone may suggest ideas for laws. Legislators write the idea as a bill. They meet to talk about the bill. Lawmakers then vote. A passed bill goes to the **governor**. The governor signs the bill into law or **vetoes** it. Legislators may change a vetoed bill and vote again.

Fun Fact:
Most state legislative branches have two parts. These parts often are called the house of representatives and the senate.

A Legislator's Job

Legislators have busy jobs. They write and study bills. Lawmakers plan how to spend state money. They also serve on committees. These groups hold meetings called hearings. At hearings, people tell lawmakers their thoughts about bills.

Fun Fact:
Many legislators have other jobs. Some legislators also work as teachers, lawyers, or police officers.

Legislators Meet with People

State legislators meet with many
people. They meet with the governor.
They meet with state leaders about bills.

Legislators meet with people in their districts. They go to town meetings. They visit schools and businesses. They listen to ideas from people in their state.

Legislatures Have Leaders

Each state legislature has leaders. Members of each legislature vote for these leaders. Leaders of the legislature are in charge of meetings. They help lawmakers work together. These leaders also meet with the governor about new laws.

Amazing But True!

Nebraska is the only state with a legislature that has one part. This part is called a senate. Nebraska's legislature had two parts for 68 years. U.S. Senator George Norris of Nebraska said a one-part legislature would save the state money. He drove across the state telling people about the idea. Norris drove so much that he wore out two sets of car tires. In 1934, Nebraska voters agreed with Norris. The new Nebraska senate first met three years later.

U.S. Senator George Norris of Nebraska

Hands On: Write Your Legislator

Legislators like to hear how children would improve their state. Share your ideas with your state legislators by writing a letter.

What You Need

pencil

paper

envelope

postage stamp

an adult to help

What You Do

1. Ask an adult to help you find addresses for your state's legislators in the newspaper or at local libraries. Addresses for all state legislators can also be found at *http://www.ncsl.org/public/leglinks.cfm.*
2. Think of something you would like to change in your school, community, or state. Ask your friends and family for their ideas.
3. Write your ideas on a piece of paper. Begin your letter with a greeting followed by your legislator's title and name.
4. Sign your letter.
5. Place the letter in an envelope.
6. Put a postage stamp on the envelope's upper right corner.
7. Address the letter.
8. Ask an adult to help mail the letter.

Glossary

bill (BIL)—a written plan for a new law

executive (eg-ZEK-yoo-tiv)—the branch of state government that makes sure laws are followed

governor (GUHV-urn-or)—the leader of a state's executive branch of government

judicial (joo-DISH-uhl)—the branch of state government that includes courts; the judicial branch explains laws.

legislative (LEH-juhs-lay-tiv)—the branch of state government that writes bills that become laws

legislator (LEH-juhs-lay-tor)—a member of the state legislative branch; legislators are often called lawmakers.

term (TERM)—a set period of time that elected leaders serve in office

veto (VEE-toh)—to stop a bill from becoming law

Read More

Giesecke, Ernestine. *State Government.* Kids' Guide. Chicago: Heinemann Library, 2000.

LeVert, Suzanne. *How States Make Laws.* Kaleidoscope. New York: Benchmark Books, 2004.

Murphy, Patricia J. *Election Day.* Rookie Read-About Holidays. New York: Children's Press, 2002.

Internet Sites

FactHound offers a safe, fun way to find Internet sites related to this book. All of the sites on FactHound have been researched by our staff.

Here's how:

1) Visit *www.facthound.com*
2) Type in this special code **0736825010** for age-appropriate sites. Or enter a search word related to this book for a more general search.
3) Click on the Fetch It button.

FactHound will fetch the best sites for you!

Index